Dear Parent:
Your child's love of reading starts here!

Every child learns to read in a different way and at his or her own speed. Some go back and forth between reading levels and read favorite books again and again. Others read through each level in order. You can help your young reader improve and become more confident by encouraging his or her own interests and abilities. From books your child reads with you to the first books he or she reads alone, there are I Can Read Books for every stage of reading:

SHARED READING
Basic language, word repetition, and whimsical illustrations, ideal for sharing with your emergent reader

BEGINNING READING
Short sentences, familiar words, and simple concepts for children eager to read on their own

READING WITH HELP
Engaging stories, longer sentences, and lar
for developing readers

READING ALONE
Complex plots, challenging vocabulary, and high-interest topics for the independent reader

I Can Read Books have introduced children to the joy of reading since 1957. Featuring award-winning authors and illustrators and a fabulous cast of beloved characters, I Can Read Books set the standard for beginning readers.

A lifetime of discovery begins with the magical words "I Can Read!"

Visit www.icanread.com for information
on enriching your child's reading experience.

Will you plant wildflowers for butterflies this year?
Then this book is dedicated to *you*!—J.B.

The National Wildlife Federation & Ranger Rick contributors: Children's
Publication Staff, Licensing Staff, and in-house naturalist David Mizejewski

Ranger Rick: I Wish I Was a Monarch Butterfly
Copyright © 2019 by National Wildlife Federation. All rights reserved.
Manufactured in U.S.A. No part of this book may be used or reproduced in any manner whatsoever without
written permission except in the case of brief quotations embodied in critical articles and reviews. For
information address HarperCollins Children's Books, a division of HarperCollins Publishers, 195 Broadway,
New York, NY 10007.
www.icanread.com
www.RangerRick.com

Library of Congress Control Number: 2018961833
ISBN 978-0-06-243223-0 (trade bdg.)—ISBN 978-0-06-243222-3 (pbk.)

Typography by Brenda E. Angelilli
19 20 LSCC 10 9 8 7 6 5 4 3 2 ❖ First Edition

I Can Read!

BEGINNING 1 READING

Ranger Rick

I Wish I Was a Monarch Butterfly

by Jennifer Bové

HARPER

An Imprint of HarperCollinsPublishers

What if you wished you were
a monarch butterfly?

Then you became a monarch.

Could you fly like a monarch?

Eat like a monarch?

Start your life as a caterpillar?

And would you want to? Find out!

Where would you live?

Monarchs spend their summers
in the United States and Canada.
They live in grasslands and gardens
where wildflowers grow.
Milkweed is their favorite plant.
In the fall, the monarchs fly south
to spend winter in California
and Mexico.

Monarch egg

How would your life begin?

Every monarch butterfly
starts life as a tiny egg.
In spring and summer,
monarch moms lay eggs
on milkweed plants.
Then they fly away.

In just a few days, the egg hatches
and a small caterpillar crawls out.
It will become a butterfly,
but it does not have wings just yet.

What would you eat as a caterpillar?

Monarch caterpillars eat only milkweed leaves.

They eat so much and grow so fast that they must shed their skin when it feels too tight.

Shedding means they crawl out of a thin layer of skin. This caterpillar is leaving its small skin behind.

Do you "shed" your clothes as you grow bigger?

How would growing up change you?

After two weeks of growing,
a caterpillar is about the size
of your index finger.

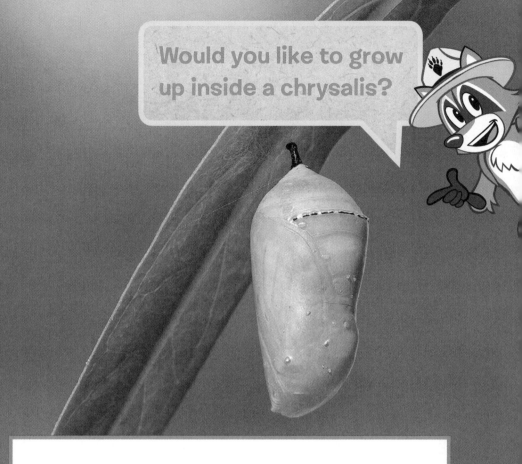

Would you like to grow up inside a chrysalis?

When a caterpillar is ready
to change into a butterfly,
it grows a hard shell.
The shell is called a chrysalis.
It hangs from a leaf or twig.

Big changes are happening
inside the chrysalis.
The caterpillar will become
a monarch butterfly
in about two weeks.

When the butterfly breaks through
the hard shell of the chrysalis,
its wings are soft and wet.
When the wings dry,
the monarch can fly.

How will you change
as you grow up?

What would you eat as a butterfly?

Adult monarchs don't eat leaves
the way caterpillars do.
They feed only on sweet liquid
from milkweed and other flowers.
This liquid is called nectar.

Do you sip juice
through a straw?

A monarch sips flower nectar
with a thin tube called a proboscis.
The proboscis is not a tongue.
It is the butterfly's mouth.

How would you wash up?

Monarchs don't need to take baths.
But they do sunbathe to warm up.
Butterflies need to be warm
in order to fly.
Butterflies spread their wings
to soak up the sun's warmth.
This is called basking.

Would you like to stay clean
without taking baths?

How would you talk?

Monarchs do not make noises.

They communicate with color.

A monarch's bright colors

tell other animals, "I'm poisonous!"

Eating a monarch will make

an animal feel sick.

Then it won't want to eat another.

Where would you sleep?

Monarchs rest in trees
or bushes at night.
In the morning, butterflies bask
in sunlight to warm up
and start a new day.

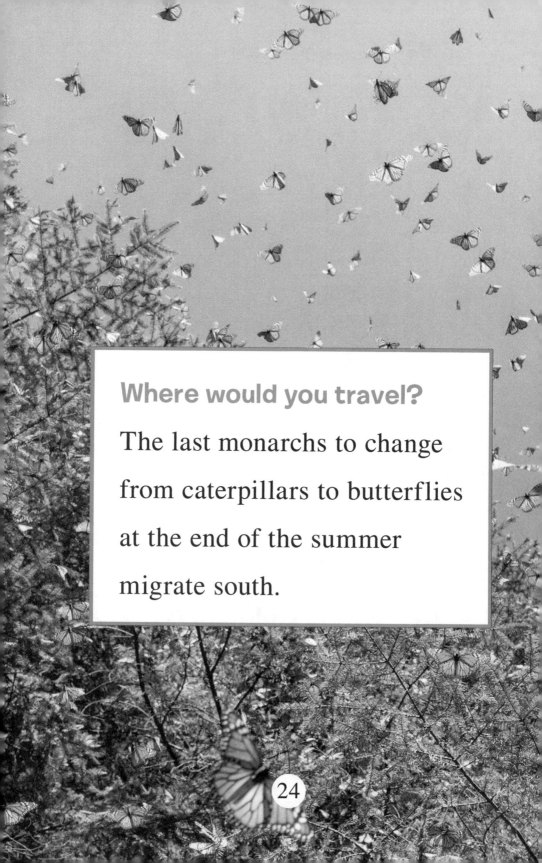

Where would you travel?

The last monarchs to change from caterpillars to butterflies at the end of the summer migrate south.

Monarchs can fly
over two thousand miles
on their fragile wings!
They face many dangers
while migrating.
It is a long and tiring trip.

Have you ever gone
on a long trip?

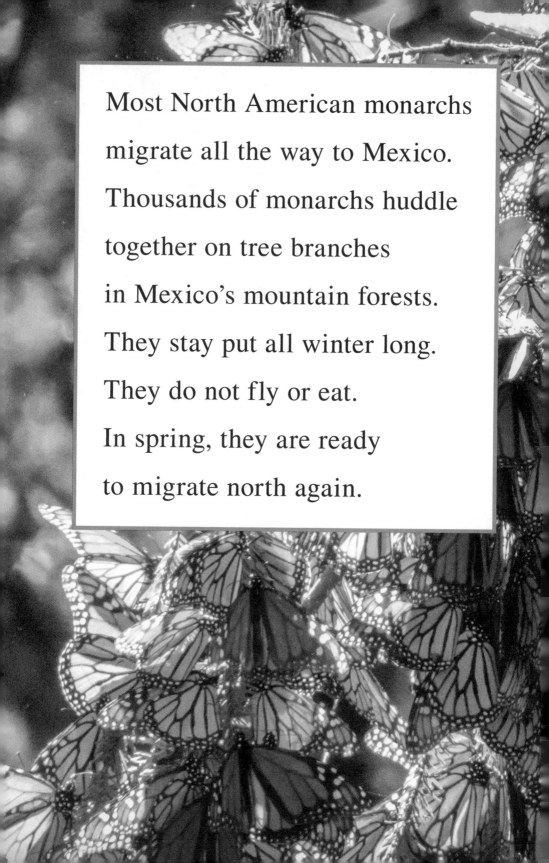

Most North American monarchs
migrate all the way to Mexico.
Thousands of monarchs huddle
together on tree branches
in Mexico's mountain forests.
They stay put all winter long.
They do not fly or eat.
In spring, they are ready
to migrate north again.

Being a monarch butterfly

could be cool for a while.

But do you want to grow wings?

Eat only nectar?

Migrate for thousands of miles?

Luckily, you don't have to.

You're not a monarch.

You're YOU!

Did You Know?

🐾 Monarch butterflies have two pairs of wings and six legs.

🐾 Monarch wings are covered with tiny scales that are brightly colored.

🐾 Male monarchs have a black spot in the center of each back wing. Females do not.

🐾 There are many fewer monarchs alive today than twenty years ago. This is because so many plants and trees that monarchs need have been cut down to make room for houses and farm fields. You can help by planting native milkweed in your yard.

Fun Zone

Make a Monarch Life Cycle Chart

What You Need:

Paper plate • Marker • Glue • Dry rice • Dry pasta: rotini, shell, and bowtie • Two leaves • Twig • Craft paint

What You Do:

- Draw one line down the center of your plate. Draw another line across the center. Now you have four sections. Label your sections with the stages of a monarch life cycle: Egg, Caterpillar, Chrysalis, and Butterfly.

- Glue a leaf onto the "Egg" section. Glue a few pieces of rice on the leaf. These are your monarch eggs.

- Glue another leaf onto the "Caterpillar" section. Glue one piece of rotini pasta on the leaf. This is your caterpillar.

- Glue a twig onto the "Chrysalis" section. Glue a piece of shell pasta so that only the small, pointy end is touching the twig. This is your hanging chrysalis.

- Glue a piece of bowtie pasta in the "Butterfly" section. This is your butterfly.

- Now paint each section to look like the pictures in this book.

31

Wild Words

Bask: to sit still with wings spread to warm up in sunlight

Butterfly: an insect with two pairs of large wings that stand up straight from its body

Caterpillar: the wormlike insect that will change into a butterfly

Chrysalis: the life phase when a caterpillar changes into a butterfly inside a hard skin

Migration: a long trip that an animal takes to a different place when seasons change

Milkweed: the most important plant to monarchs. It's the only plant monarch caterpillars can eat. Monarch butterflies also drink milkweed nectar.

Monarch: a large butterfly with orange and black wings

Nectar: the sweet liquid inside flowers

Proboscis: a butterfly's mouth

Shedding: the process of removing old skin as a caterpillar grows

Dig Deeper

WANT TO FIND OUT EVEN MORE ABOUT MONARCHS?

Check out the Ranger Rick website: www.RangerRick.com Or visit www.nwf.org/wildlife-guide SEARCH: monarch

Photography from the archives of the National Wildlife Federation by Dulce Benetti
Photography © Getty Images by Leekris, Liliboas, Herreid, SusanWoodImages, Jim Simmen, Cyndi Monaghan, Dossyl, Lisa5201, Mathisa_s, Kerri Wile, 8ran, Willowpix, Emkaplin, Sylvan Cordier, JHVEPhoto, AlpamayoPhoto